C.S.LEWIS

~ on ~

LOVE

C. S. LEWIS

~ *on* ~

LOVE

Compiled by

LESLEY WALMSLEY

THOMAS NELSON PUBLISHERS
Nashville

Published in Nashville, Tennessee
by Thomas Nelson, Inc.

1 2 3 4 5 6 – 03 02 01 00 99 98

Extracts from C.S. Lewis's works © C.S. Lewis Pte Ltd.
Introduction and compilation © 1998 Lesley Walmsley
Cover illustration © 1998 Sarah Young

Produced for Thomas Nelson, Inc. by Godsfield Press

Designed and produced by
THE BRIDGEWATER BOOK COMPANY LTD

Picture research by Jane Moore

The Catalog Card Number is on file
with the Library of Congress.

ISBN 0 7852 7098 1

Printed in Hong Kong

CONDITIONS OF SALE

Contents

Introduction

L *ove is one of the most talked about, written about, dreamt about topics in the world. It has all kinds of facets, and whether you have enough love of one kind or another, not enough, or even, in some cases, too much, it is always of vital interest to you and to those who care about you. The giving and receiving of love is one of the things that can make life truly happy.*

C.S. Lewis

This selection from the writings of C.S. Lewis tries to cover the subject of love, but although to anyone reading his works it is clear that Christian love underlies his whole life, it has sometimes been difficult to extract this aspect from them. On the subject of faith Lewis wrote clearly and after much thought, so that, as a teacher, he could help others to find their own faith. But love was so basic to his life that he was not so explicit, and tended more to mention it in passing than to provide long discussions about it.

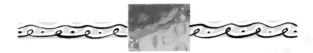

Clive Staples (Jack) Lewis was born in Belfast on 29 November 1898, the younger of two brothers, sons of a rather starchy lawyer who seems to have found communicating with them difficult, although he did try. When their mother died, unable to understand the grief of the adults around them, Jack and his brother Warren (Warnie) turned increasingly to each other for solace and friendship, a brotherly love that was to last all their lives, until Jack's death in 1963. Sent away to boarding schools in England, each remained a firm rock for the other. After school Warnie was away again, this time in the army, and after a short stint serving in the First World War himself, Jack went back to Oxford to continue his studies.

C S Lewis's mother

Here he was in his element. He enjoyed the companionship of lecturers and undergraduates alike, in a very masculine world, although he also had the problems of trying to run a household

when he took over care for the mother and sister of his late friend, Paddy Moore. Much has been written of his relationship with Mrs Moore, but whatever the truth of it, Jack Lewis showed great tolerance and patience in it for many years.

In 1952 he made the acquaintance of Joy Davidman Gresham, an American with whom he had corresponded for two years. After her divorce and return to England in 1953, Jack and Warnie invited her and her two sons to visit them at their home, The Kilns, and a great affection developed between them all. When Joy's permit to remain in England expired, she and Jack went through a civil marriage ceremony in April 1956 in order that she might stay. At first it was no more than a convenient arrangement between two friends, but friendship turned to love, although they did not live as man and wife or regard themselves as married in the sight of God until their religious ceremony in March 1957. Lewis described this time with Joy as the happiest of his life.

But then Joy developed cancer, and they shared all the hopes and fears of illness, remission, illness again and finally her death. Jack's book A Grief Observed, written after Joy's death, is a classic which has brought comfort to thousands of people grieving for loved ones. When they married, Jack was a middle-aged man, comfortable in the traditions and thinking of

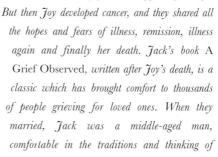

Helen Joy
Davidman

university life, and recognized as 'a confirmed bachelor', yet the few years they had together brought him another kind of love from those he had already known – and it also brought him two stepsons, David and Douglas, for whom he was to care until his death.

Magdalen College, Oxford

C.S. Lewis experienced love of many kinds – as a son and brother, as a husband and a stepfather, and above all as a staunch and long-standing friend. He was also academically well-versed in the medieval Romantic literature which was his main subject. He let love of many kinds run right through his whole life. He took seriously the command of Jesus that we should love one another.

Lewis was writing in a very different world from the one in which we live today. In particular, as women were then only beginning to exert much influence outside the home, it was quite normal to refer to 'a man who', whereas today we would use more inclusive language. Lewis respected everyone for what they were, and if he were writing now I am sure that this would be reflected in his style. But he is not, and I have decided to leave his thoughts as he expressed them.

I hope these extracts will give you some idea of C.S. Lewis's thinking about love in all its aspects, and that you will find even more pleasure by reading the books from which they are taken.

≈ LESLEY WALMSLEY

Love and kindness

There is kindness in Love: but Love and Kindness are not coterminous, and when kindness... is separated from the other elements of Love, it involves a certain fundamental indifference to its object, and even something like contempt of it... Kindness, merely as such, cares not whether its object becomes good or bad, provided only that it escapes suffering. As Scripture points out, it is bastards who are spoiled: the legitimate sons, who are to carry on the family tradition, are punished (Hebrews 12:8). It is for people whom we care nothing about that we demand happiness on any terms: with our friends, our lovers, our children, we are exacting and would rather see them suffer much than be happy in contemptible and estranging modes...

When Christianity says that God loves man, it means that God *loves* man: not that He has some 'disinterested', because really indifferent, concern for our welfare, but that, in awful and surprising truth, we are the objects of His love. You asked for a loving God: you have one. The great spirit you so lightly invoked, the 'lord of terrible

aspect', is present: not a senile benevolence that drowsily wishes you to be happy in your own way, not the cold philanthropy of a conscientious magistrate, nor the care of a host who feels responsible for the comfort of his guests, but the consuming fire Himself, the Love that made the worlds, persistent as the artist's love for his work and despotic as a man's love for a child, jealous, inexorable, exacting as love between the sexes.

≈ *THE PROBLEM OF PAIN*

The Madonna with St Anne, LEONARDO DA VINCI (1452–1519)

Gift-love and Need-love

Every human love, at its height, has a tendency to claim for itself a divine authority. Its voice tends to sound as if it were the will of God Himself. It tells us not to count the cost, it demands of us a total commitment, it attempts to override all other claims and insinuates that any action which is sincerely done 'for love's sake' is thereby lawful and even meritorious. That erotic love and love of one's country may thus attempt to 'become gods' is generally recognized. But family affection may do the same. So, in a different way, may friendship…

Now it must be noticed that the natural loves make this blasphemous claim not when they are in their worst, but when they are in

their best, natural condition; when they are what our grandfathers called 'pure' or 'noble'... A faithful and genuinely self-sacrificing passion will speak to us with what seems the voice of God...

Let us here make no mistake. Our Gift-loves are really God-like; and among our Gift-loves those are most God-like which are most boundless and unwearied in giving. All the things the poets say about them are true. Their joy, their energy, their patience, their readiness to forgive, their desire for the good of the beloved – all this is a real and all but adorable image of the Divine life. In its presence we are right to thank God 'who has given such power to men'. We may say, quite truly and in an intelligible sense, that those who love greatly are 'near' to God.

≈ *THE FOUR LOVES*

Holidays,
HARRY WATSON (1871–1936)

Affection is the humblest love

ffection… is the humblest love. It gives itself no airs. People can be proud of being 'in love', or of friendship. Affection is modest – even furtive and shame-faced. Once when I had remarked on the affection quite

Arthur Greeves

often found between cat and dog, my friend replied, 'Yes. But I bet no dog would ever confess it to the other dogs.' That is at least a good caricature of much human affection. 'Let homely faces stay at home,' says Comus. Now affection has a very homely face. So have many of those for whom we feel it. It is no proof of our refinement or perceptiveness that we love them; nor that they love us…

Affection would not be affection if it was loudly and frequently expressed; to produce it in public is like getting your household furniture out for a move. It did very well in its place, but it looks shabby or tawdry or grotesque in the sunshine. Affection almost slinks or seeps through our lives. It lives with humble, un-dress, private things; soft slippers, old clothes, old jokes, the thump of a sleepy dog's tail on the kitchen floor...

To make a friend is not the same as to become affectionate. But when your friend has become an old friend, all

Lewis and friends at the Trout Inn, Oxford

those things about him which had originally nothing to do with the friendship become familiar and dear with familiarity...

≈ *THE FOUR LOVES*

Tenderness came over me again

I felt as, I suppose, a tortured prisoner feels when they dash water in his face to rouse him from his faint, and the truth, worse than all his fantasies, becomes clear and hard and unmistakable again around him… I would have killed Psyche rather than leave her to the heat or hunger of a monster. Now again I made a deep resolve. I was half frightened when I perceived what I was resolving. 'So it might come even to that,' my heart said; even to killing her (Bardia had already taught me the straight thrust, and where to strike). Then my tenderness came over me again, and I cried, never more bitterly, till I could not tell whether it was tears or rain that had most drenched my veil… And in that tenderness I even asked myself why I should save her from the Brute, or warn her against the Brute, or meddle with the matter at all. 'She is happy,' said my heart. 'Whether it's madness or a god or a monster, or whatever it is, she is happy. You have seen that for yourself. She is ten times happier, there in the mountain, than you could ever make her. Leave her alone.'…

Hunter and Courting Couple,
ILLUSTRATION FROM "ROMAN DE LA ROSE" (1567)

My heart did not conquer me. I perceived now that
there is a love deeper than theirs who seek only the
happiness of their beloved... My hand went back to the
sword. Psyche should not – least of all contentedly –
make sport for a demon.

≈ *TILL WE HAVE FACES*

Head of an Old Lady, GUSTAV KLIMT (1862–1918)

An ageing woman

Four very slender pillars held up the painted roof and between them hung a lamp that was a marvel of goldsmith's work. Beneath it, seated with her back against one of the pillars, a woman, no longer young, sat with her distaff, spinning; as a great lady might sit in her own house a thousand miles away from the war.

Yellowhead had been in ambushes. He knew what it costs even a trained man to be still on the brink of deadly danger. He thought, 'That woman must have the blood of gods in her.' He resolved he would ask her where Helen was to be found. He would ask her courteously.

She looked up and stopped her spinning but still she did not move.

'The child,' she said in a low voice. 'Is she still alive? Is she well?' Then, helped by the voice, he recognized her. And with the first second of his recognition all that had made the very shape of his mind for eleven years came tumbling down in irretrievable ruin. Neither that jealousy nor that lust, that rage nor that tenderness, could ever be revived. There was nothing inside him appropriate to what he saw. For a moment there was nothing inside him at all.

For he had never dreamed she would be like this; never dreamed that the flesh would have gathered under her chin, that the face would be so plump and yet so drawn, that there would be grey hair at her temples and wrinkles at the corners of her eyes. Even her height was less than he remembered. The smooth glory of her skin which once made her seem to cast a light from her arms and shoulders was all gone. An ageing woman; a sad, patient, composed woman, asking for her daughter; for their daughter.

≈ 'AFTER TEN YEARS'

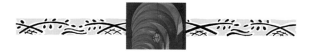

Friendship

To the Ancients, friendship seemed the happiest and most fully human of all loves; the crown of life and the school of virtue. The modern world, in comparison, ignores it... How has this come about?

The first and most obvious answer is that few value it because few experience it... Friendship is – in a sense not at all derogatory to it – the least *natural* of loves; the least instinctive, organic, biological, gregarious and necessary... Without Eros none of us would have been begotten, and without Affection none of us would have been reared; but we can live and breed without Friendship. The species, biologically considered, has no need of it...

In some ways nothing is less like a Friendship than a love affair... Above all, Eros (while it lasts) is necessarily between two only. But two, far from being the necessary number for Friendship, is not even the best... Two friends delight to be joined by a third, and three by a fourth, if only the newcomer is qualified to become a real friend... Of course the scarcity of kindred souls...sets limits to the enlargement of the circle; but within those limits we possess each friend not less but

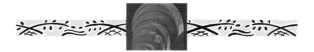

more as the number of those with whom we share him increases. In this, Friendship exhibits a glorious 'nearness by resemblance' to Heaven itself where the very multitude of the blessed (which no man can number) increases the fruition which each has of God. For every soul, seeing Him in her own way, doubtless communicates that unique vision to all the rest. That, says an old author, is why the seraphim in Isaiah's vision are crying 'Holy, Holy, Holy' *to one another* (Isaiah 6:3). The more we thus share the Heavenly Bread between us, the more we shall all have.

≈ *THE FOUR LOVES*

The Last Supper, BARTOLOMEO CARDUCCIO (1554–1608)

Eros

By *Eros* I mean of course that state which we call 'being in love'; or, if you prefer, that kind of love which lovers are 'in'… The times and places in which marriage depends on Eros are in a small minority. Most of our ancestors were married off in early youth to partners chosen by their parents on grounds that had nothing to do with Eros… honest Christian husbands and wives, obeying their fathers and mothers, discharging to one another their 'marriage debt', and bringing up families in the fear of the Lord…

It has not pleased God that the distinction between a sin and a duty should turn on fine feelings. This act, like any other, is justified (or not) by far more prosaic and

definable criteria; by the keeping or breaking of promises, by justice or injustice, by charity or selfishness, by obedience or disobedience…

It is in the grandeur of Eros that the seeds of danger are concealed. He has spoken like a god. His total

commitment, his reckless disregard of happiness, his transcendence of self-regard, sound like a message from the eternal world…

And yet it cannot, just as it stands, be the voice of God Himself. For Eros, speaking with that very grandeur and displaying that very transcendence of self, may urge to evil as well as to good.

≈ *THE FOUR LOVES*

Love at the Spring of Youth,
GIOVANNI SEGANTINI (1858–99)

My noble bride

With tambourines of amber, queens
    In rose and lily garlanded
Shall go beside my noble bride
    With dance and din and harmony,
And sabre clash and tabor crash
    And lantern light and torches flash
On shield and helmet, plume and sash,
    The flower of all my armoury…

What flame before our chamber door
    Shines in on love's security?
Fiercer than day, its piercing ray
    Pours round us unendurably.
It's Aphrodite's saffron light,
    And Jove's monarchal presence bright
And Genius burning through the night
    The torch of man's futurity.

For her the swords of furthest lords
    Have flashed in fields ethereal;
The dynasts seven incline from heaven

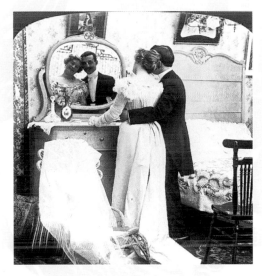

Reflection, R.Y. YOUNG

With glad regard and serious,
And ponder there beyond our air
The infinite unborn, and care
For history, while the mortal pair
Lie drowned in dreaming weariness.

≈ 'THE SMALL MAN ORDERS
HIS WEDDING'

Topiary Garden, LIZ WRIGHT

Unless His grace comes down...

William Morris wrote a poem called 'Love is enough', and someone is said to have reviewed it briefly in the words 'It isn't'... The natural loves are not self-sufficient. Something else, at first vaguely described as 'decency and common sense', but later revealed as goodness, and finally as the whole Christian life in one particular relation, must come to the help of the mere feeling if the feeling is to be kept sweet.

To say this is not to belittle the natural loves but to indicate where their real glory lies. It is no disparagement to a garden to say that it will not fence and weed itself, nor prune its own fruit trees, nor roll and cut its own lawns. A garden is a good thing but that is not the sort of goodness it has. It will remain a garden,

as distinct from a wilderness, only if someone does all these things to it. Its real glory is of a different kind. The very fact that it needs constant weeding and pruning bears witness to that glory. It teems with life...

When God planted a garden He set a man over it and set the man under Himself. When He planted the garden of our nature and caused the flowering, fruiting loves to grow there, He set our will to 'dress' them. Compared with them it is dry and cold. And unless His grace comes down, like the rain and the sunshine, we shall use this tool to little purpose. But its laborious – and largely negative – services are indispensable. If they were needed when the garden was still Paradisal, how much more now when the soil has gone sour and the weeds seem to thrive on it best? But heaven forbid we should work in the spirit of prigs and Stoics. While we hack and prune we know very well that what we are hacking and pruning is big with a splendour and vitality which our rational will could never of itself have supplied. To liberate that splendour, to let it become fully what it is trying to be, to have tall trees instead of scrubby tangles, and sweet apples instead of crabs, is part of our purpose.

≈ *THE FOUR LOVES*

[27]

'Being in love'

What we call 'being in love' is a glorious state, and, in several ways, good for us. It helps to make us generous and courageous, it opens our eyes not only to the beauty of the beloved but to all beauty, and it subordinates (especially at first) our merely animal sexuality; in that sense, love is the great conqueror of lust. No one in his senses would deny that being in love is far better than either common sensuality or cold self-centredness. But, as I said before, 'the most dangerous thing you can do is to take any one impulse of our own nature and set it up as the thing you ought to follow at all costs'. Being in love is a good thing, but it is not the best thing. There are many things below it, but there are also things above it.

You cannot make it the basis of a whole life. It is a noble feeling, but it is still a feeling...

Knowledge can last, principles can last, habits can last; but feelings come and go... But, of course, ceasing to be 'in love' need not mean ceasing to love. Love in this second sense – love as distinct from 'being in love' – is not merely a feeling. It is a deep unity, maintained by the will and deliberately strengthened by habit; reinforced by (in Christian marriages) the grace which

both partners ask, and receive, from God... 'Being in love' first moved them to promise fidelity: this quieter love enables them to keep the promise. It is on this love that the engine of marriage is run: being in love was the explosion that started it.

≈ *MERE CHRISTIANITY*

Marsillo and his Wife,
LORENZO LOTTO (c.1400–1556)

Sex

O h for Mercy's sake. Not you too! Why, just because I raise an objection to your parallel between prayer and a man making love to his own wife, must you trot out all the rigmarole about the 'holiness' of sex and start lecturing me as if I were a Manichaean? I know that in most circles nowadays one need only mention sex to set everyone in the room emitting this gas. But, I did hope, not you. Didn't I make it plain that I objected to your image solely on the ground of its nonchalance, or presumption?

I'm not saying anything against (or for) 'sex'. Sex in itself cannot be moral or immoral any more than gravitation or nutrition. The sexual behaviour of human beings can. And like their economic, or political, or agricultural, or parental, or filial behaviour, it is sometimes good and sometimes bad. And the sexual act, when lawful – which means chiefly when consistent with good faith and charity – can, like all other merely natural acts… be done to the glory of God, and will then be holy. And like other natural acts it is sometimes so done, and sometimes not.

≈ *PRAYER: LETTERS TO MALCOLM*

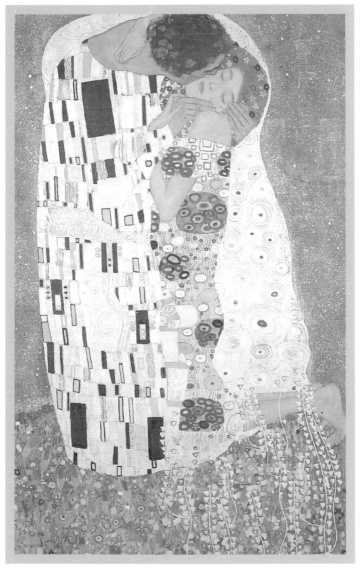

The Kiss, GUSTAV KLIMT (1862–1918)

Christian marriage

The Christian idea of marriage is based on Christ's words that a man and wife are to be regarded as a single organism – for that is what the words 'one flesh' would be in modern English. And the Christians believe that when He said this He was not expressing a sentiment but stating a fact – just as one is stating a fact when one says that a lock and its key are one mechanism, or that a violin and a bow are one musical instrument. The inventor of the human machine was telling us that its two halves, the male and the female, were made to be combined together in pairs, not simply on the sexual level, but totally combined...

The monstrosity of sexual intercourse outside marriage is that those who indulge in it are trying to isolate one kind of union (the sexual) from all other kinds of union which were intended to go along with it and make up the total union. The Christian attitude does not mean that there is anything wrong about sexual pleasure, any more than about the pleasure of eating. It means that you must not isolate that pleasure and try to get it by itself...

≈ *MERE CHRISTIANITY*

*The Marriage of St George
and Princess Sabra,*
Dante Gabriel Rossetti
(1828–82)

Remaining married

The idea that 'being in love' is the only reason for remaining married really leaves no room for marriage as a contract or promise at all. If love is the whole thing, then the promise can add nothing; and if it adds nothing, then it should not be made. The curious thing is that lovers themselves, while they remain really in love, know this better than those who talk abut love. As Chesterton pointed out, those who are in love have a natural inclination to bind themselves by promises... The Christian law is not forcing upon the passion of love something which is foreign to that passion's own nature: it is demanding that lovers should take seriously something which their passion of itself impels them to do...

And, of course, the promise, made when I am in love and because I am in love, to be true to the beloved as long as I live, commits me to being true even if I cease to be in love. A promise must be about things that I can do, about actions: no one can promise to go on feeling in a certain way. He might as well promise never to have a headache or always to feel hungry. But what, it may be

Madonna with Cat, Leonardo da Vinci (1452–1519)

asked, is the use of keeping two people together if they are no longer in love? There are several sound, social reasons: to provide a home for their children, to protect the woman (who has probably sacrificed or damaged her own career by getting married) from being dropped whenever the man is tired of her... There ought to be two distinct kinds of marriage: one governed by the State with rules enforced on all citizens, the other governed by the Church with rules enforced on her by her own members. The distinction ought to be quite sharp, so that a man knows which couples are married in a Christian sense and which are not.

≈ *MERE CHRISTIANITY*

Her absence

At first I was afraid of going to places where H. and I had been happy – our favourite pub, our favourite wood. But I decided to do it at once – like sending a pilot up again as soon as possible after he's had a crash. Unexpectedly, it makes no difference. Her absence is no more emphatic in those places than anywhere else. It's not local at all... The act of living is different all through. Her absence is like the sky, spread over everything.

Helen Joy Davidman

But no, that is not quite accurate. There is one place where her absence comes locally home to me, and it is a place I can't avoid. I mean my own body. It had such a different importance while it was the body of H.'s lover. Now it's like an empty house...

I am thinking about her nearly always. Thinking of the H. facts – real words, looks, laughs, and actions of

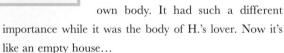

hers. But it is my own mind that selects and groups them. Already, less than a month after her death, I can feel the slow, insidious beginning of a process that will make the H. I think of into a more and more imaginary woman. Founded on fact, no doubt, I shall put in nothing fictitious (or I hope I shan't). But won't the

C.S. Lewis

composition inevitably become more and more my own? The reality is no longer there to check me, to pull me up short, as the real H. so often did, so unexpectedly, by being so thoroughly herself and not me.

The most precious gift that marriage gave me was of something very close and intimate yet all the time unmistakably other, resistant – in a word, real. Is all that work to be undone? Is what I shall still call H. to sink back horribly into being not much more than one of my old bachelor pipe-dreams? Oh my dear, my dear, come back for one moment and drive that miserable phantom away. Oh God, God, why did you take such trouble to force this creature out of its shell if it is now doomed to crawl back – to be sucked back into it?

≈ *A GRIEF OBSERVED*

[37]

God, man and love

Some writers use the word 'charity' to describe not only Christian love between human beings, but also God's love for man and man's love for God. About the second of these two, people are often worried. They are told they ought to love God. They cannot find any such feeling in themselves. What are they to do? The answer is the same as before. Act as if you did. Do not sit trying to manufacture feelings. Ask yourself, 'If I were sure that I loved God, what would I do?' When you have found the answer, go and do it...

Christian Love, either towards God or towards man, is an affair of the will. If we are trying to do His will we are obeying the commandment 'Thou shalt love the Lord thy God'. He will give us feelings of love if He pleases. We cannot create them for ourselves, and we must not demand them as a right. But the great thing to remember is that, though our feelings come and go, His love for us does not. It is not wearied by our sins, or our indifference; and, therefore, it is quite relentless in its determination that we shall be cured of those sins, at whatever cost to us, at whatever cost to Him.

≈ *MERE CHRISTIANITY*

Christian love
for our neighbours

Do not waste time bothering whether you 'love' your neighbour; act as if you did. As soon as we do this we find one of the great secrets. When you are behaving as if you loved someone, you will presently come to love him. If you injure someone you dislike, you will find yourself disliking him more. If you do him a good turn, you will find yourself disliking him less. There is, indeed, one exception. If you do him a good turn, not to please God and obey the law of charity, but to show him what a fine forgiving chap you are, and to put him in your debt, and then sit down to wait for his 'gratitude', you will probably be disappointed. (People are not fools: they have a very quick eye for anything like showing off, or patronage.) But whenever we do good to another self, just because it is a self, made (like us) by God, and desiring its own happiness as we desire ours, we shall have learned to love it a little more or, at least, to dislike it less.

≈ *MERE CHRISTIANITY*

Motherhood
of a different kind

Only partly do I remember the unbearable beauty of her face. 'Is it?... Is it?' I whispered to my guide.

'Not at all,' said he. 'It's someone ye'll never have heard of. Her name on earth was Sarah Smith and she lived at Golders Green.'

'She seems to be... well, a person of particular importance?'

'Aye. She is one of the great ones. Ye have heard that fame in this country and fame on Earth are two quite different things.'...

'And who are all these young men and women on each side?'

'They are her sons and daughters.'

'She must have had a very large family, Sir.'

'Every young man or boy that met her became her son – even if it was only the boy that brought the meat to her back door. Every girl that met her was her daughter.'

'Isn't that a bit hard on their own parents?'

Madonna and Child, GIOVANNI BELLINI (1430–1516)

'No. There *are* those that steal other people's children. But her motherhood was of a different kind. Those on whom it fell went back to their natural parents loving them more. Few men looked on her without becoming, in a certain fashion, her lovers. But it was the kind of love that made them not less true, but truer, to their own wives… It is like when you throw a stone into a pool and the concentric waves spread out further and further. Who knows where it will end?… But already there is joy enough in the little finger of a great saint such as yonder lady to waken all the dead things of the universe into life.'

≈ *THE GREAT DIVORCE*

Rejecting the claims of the Self

There are three kinds of people in the world. The first class is of those who live simply for their own sake and pleasure, regarding Man and Nature as so much raw material to be cut up into whatever shape may serve them. In the second class are those who acknowledge some other claim upon them – the will of God, the categorical imperative, or the good of society – and honestly try to pursue their own interests no further

than this claim will allow. They try to surrender to the higher claim as much as it demands, like men paying a tax, but hope, like other taxpayers, that what is left over will be enough for them to live on... But the third class is of those who can say with St Paul that for them 'to live is Christ'. These people have got rid of the tiresome business of adjusting the rival claims of Self and God by the simple expedient of rejecting the claims of the Self altogether. The old egoistic will has been turned round, reconditioned, and made into a new thing. The will of Christ no longer limits theirs; it is theirs. All their time, in belonging to Him, belongs also to them, for they are His...

The price of Christ is something, in a way, much easier than moral effort – it is to want Him. It is true that the wanting itself would be beyond our power but for one fact. The world is so built that, to help us desert our own satisfactions, they desert us. War and trouble and finally old age take from us one by one all those things that the natural Self hoped for at its setting out. Begging is our only wisdom, and want in the end makes it easier for us to be beggars. Even on those terms the Mercy will receive us.

≈ 'THREE KINDS OF MEN'

Forgiveness

Everyone says forgiveness is a lovely idea, until they have something to forgive… One might start with forgiving one's husband or wife, or parents or children… for something they have done or said in the last week. That will probably keep us busy for the moment. And secondly, we might try to understand exactly what loving your neighbour as yourself means. I have to love him as I love myself. Well, how exactly do I love myself?…

Do I think well of myself, think myself a nice chap? Well, I am afraid I sometimes do (and those are, no doubt, my worst moments) but that is not why I love myself. In fact it is the other way round: my self-love makes me think myself nice, but thinking myself nice is not why I love myself. So loving my enemies does not apparently mean thinking them nice either. That is an enormous relief…

I remember Christian teachers telling me long ago that I must hate a bad man's actions, but not hate the bad man: or, as they would say, hate the sin but not the sinner.

For a long time I used to think this a silly, straw-splitting distinction: how could you hate what a man did and not hate the man? But years later it occurred to me that there was one man to whom I had been doing this all my life — namely myself. However much I might dislike my own cowardice or conceit or greed, I went on loving myself. There had never been the slightest difficulty about it. In fact the very reason why I hated the things was that I loved the man. Just because I loved myself, I was sorry to find that I was the sort of man who did those things.

≈ *MERE CHRISTIANITY*

Christ and the Woman Taken in Adultery,
PIETER BRUEGHEL (1515–69)

Forgiving and excusing

We believe that God forgives us our sins; but also that He will not do so unless we forgive other people their sins against us. There is no doubt about the second part of this statement. It is in the Lord's Prayer: it was emphatically stated by Our Lord... He doesn't say that we are to forgive other people's sins provided they are not too frightful, or provided there are extenuating circumstances, or anything of that sort. We are to forgive them all, however spiteful, however mean, however often they are repeated. If we don't, we shall be forgiven none of our own...

I find that when I think I am asking God to forgive me I am often in reality... asking Him not to forgive me but to excuse me. But there is all the difference in the world between forgiving and excusing. Forgiveness says 'Yes, you have done this thing, but I accept your apology, I will never hold it against you and everything between us two will be exactly as it was before.' But excusing says 'I see that you couldn't help it or didn't mean it, you weren't really to blame.' If one was not really to blame then there is nothing to forgive. In that sense forgiveness and excusing are almost opposites...

Real forgiveness means looking steadily at the sin, the sin that is left over without any excuse, after all allowances have been made, and seeing it in all its horror, dirt, meanness and malice, and nevertheless being wholly reconciled to the man who has done it... To be a Christian means to forgive the inexcusable, because God has forgiven the inexcusable in you.

≈ 'ON FORGIVENESS'

Room in New York, EDWARD HOPPER (1882–1967)

[47]

Self-love

Now the Self can be regarded in two ways. On the one hand, it is God's creature, an occasion of love and rejoicing; now, indeed, hateful in condition, but to be pitied and healed. On the other hand, it is that one self of all others which is called *I* and *me,* and which on that ground puts forward an irrational claim to preference. This claim is to be not only hated, but simply killed... The Christian must wage endless war against the clamour of the ego as ego: but he loves and approves selves as such, though not their sins...

The very self-love which he has to reject is to him a specimen of how he ought to feel to all selves; and he may hope that when he has truly learned (which will hardly be in this life) to love his neighbour as himself, he may then be able to love himself as his neighbour: that is, with charity instead of partiality.

The other kind of self-hatred, on the contrary, hates selves as such. It begins by accepting the special value of the particular self called me, then, wounded in its pride to find that such a darling object should be so disappointing, it seeks revenge, first upon that self, then on all. Deeply egoistic, but now with an inverted egoism, it uses the revealing argument, 'I don't spare myself' – with the implication 'then *a fortiori* I need not spare others'…

The wrong asceticism torments the self: the right kind kills the selfness. We must die daily: but it is better to love the self than to love nothing, and to pity the self than to pity no one.

≈ 'TWO WAYS WITH THE SELF'

He himself wept not

Then the cold hours began their march again, not worse,
    Not better, never-ending. And that night he came,
Out of the doorway's curtained darkness to the flame
    Of candlelight and firelight. And the curtains fell
Behind him, and they stood alone, with all to tell,
    Not like that Launcelot tangled in the boughs of May
Long since, nor like the Guinever he kissed that day,
    But he was pale, with pity in his face writ wide,
And she a haggard woman, holding to her side
    A pale hand pressed, asking 'What is it?' Slowly then
He came to her and took her by the hand, as men
    Take tenderly a daughter's or a mother's hand
To whom they bring bad news she will not understand.
    So Launcelot led the Queen and made her sit: and all
This time he saw her shoulders move and her tears fall,
    And he himself wept not, but sighed. Then, like a man
Who ponders, in the fire he gazed; and so began
    Presently, looking always in the fire, the tale
Of his adventures seeking for the Holy Grail.

≈ 'LAUNCELOT'

Lancelot and Guinevere, GUSTAVE DORÉ (1832–83)

Good manners

There is a distinction between public and domestic courtesy. The root principle of both is the same: 'that no one give any kind of preference to himself.' But the more public the occasion, the more our obedience to this principle has been 'taped' or formalized. There are 'rules' of good manners…

The more intimate the occasion, the less the formalization; but not therefore the less need of courtesy. On the contrary, Affection at its best practises a courtesy which is incomparably more subtle, sensitive and deep than the public kind. In public a ritual would do. At home you must have the reality which that ritual represented, or else the deafening triumphs of the greatest egoist present… Those who leave their manners

behind them when they come home
from the dance or the sherry party
have no real courtesy even there. They
were merely aping those who did.

'We can say anything to one
another.' The truth behind this is that
Affection at its best can say whatever Affection at its best
wishes to say, regardless of the rules that govern public
courtesy; for Affection at its best wishes neither to wound
nor to humiliate nor to domineer... You can do anything
in the right tone and at
the right moment – the
tone and moment which
are not intended to, and
will not, hurt. The better
the Affection the more
unerringly it knows which
these are (every love has
its art of love).

≈ *THE FOUR LOVES*

The Roof Terrace at Potsdam,
LOTTE LASERSTEIN

The pleasure of praise

When I began to look into this matter I was shocked to find such different Christians as Milton, Johnson and Thomas Aquinas taking heavenly glory quite frankly in the sense of fame or good report. But not fame conferred by our fellow creatures – fame with God, approval or (I might say) 'appreciation' by God. And then, when I had thought it over, I saw that this view was scriptural; nothing can eliminate from the parable the divine *accolade*, 'Well done, thou good and faithful servant.' With that, a good deal of what I had been thinking all my life fell down like a house of cards. I suddenly remembered that no one can enter heaven except as a child; and nothing is so obvious in a child – not in a conceited child, but in a good child – as its great and undisguised pleasure in being praised...

I am not forgetting how horribly this most innocent desire is parodied in our human ambitions, or how very quickly, in my own experience, the lawful pleasure of praise from those whom it was my duty to

Jack Lewis aged five

The Lewis family at Home, 1901

please turns into the deadly poison of self-admiration. But I thought I could detect a moment – a very, very short moment – before this happened, during which the satisfaction of having pleased those whom I rightly loved and rightly feared was pure. And that is enough to raise our thoughts to what may happen when the redeemed soul, beyond all hope and nearly beyond belief, learns at last that she has pleased Him whom she was created to please. There will be no room for vanity then. She will be free from the miserable illusion that it is her doing. With no taint of what we should now call self-approval she will most innocently rejoice in the thing which God has made her to be, and the moment which heals her old inferiority complex for ever will also drown her pride deeper than Prospero's book. Perfect humility dispenses with modesty. If God is satisfied with the work, the work may be satisfied with itself.

≈ 'THE WEIGHT OF GLORY'

A kind of love

*Magdalen College,
Oxford*

I had a really delightful experience some weeks ago. An old pupil of mine, one Wood, came to spend a night with me. When I was his tutor he had been a curiously naive, almost neurotic youth, who was always in love and other troubles... Altogether an appealing, but somewhat ridiculous young man. When he went down he was compelled against his will to go into his father's business: and for a year (or) so I got letters from him, and accounts of him from common friends, which seemed to show that he was settling down into a permanent state of self-pity.

You can imagine how pleased I was to find that he had got over this: but above all – that is why I am telling the story – to find that his whole support is Romantic reading in those precious evening hours 'after business'... He quoted bits of Middle English poems which he had read with me for the exam. They were mere drudgery to him at the time, but now, in memory, they delight him...

In fact as I sat talking to him, hearing his not very articulate, but unmistakable, attempts to express his pleasure, I really felt as if I were meeting *our* former selves... Of course there was an element of vanity on my side... But in the main the pleasure was a spiritual one – a kind of love. It is difficult, without being sentimental, to say how extraordinarily *beautiful* – ravishing – I found the sight of someone just at that point which you and I remember so well... I suppose it is this pleasure which fathers always are hoping to get, and very seldom do get, from their sons.

≈ *THEY STAND TOGETHER*

The Lewis family, 1911

Bereavement

Children suffer not (I think) less than their elders, but differently. For us boys the real bereavement had happened before our mother died. We lost her gradually as she was gradually withdrawn from our life into the hands of nurses and delirium and morphia, and as our whole existence changed into something alien and menacing, as the house became full of strange smells and midnight noises and sinister whispered conversations… If I may trust to my

C S Lewis's mother

own experience, the sight of adult misery and adult terror has an effect on children which is merely paralysing and alienating. Perhaps it was our fault. Perhaps if we had been better children we might have lightened our father's sufferings at this time. We certainly did not... We were coming, my brother and I, to rely more and more exclusively on each other for all that made life bearable; to have confidence only in each other... We drew daily closer together (that was the good result) – two frightened urchins huddled for warmth in a bleak world.

≈ *SURPRISED BY JOY*

Go down to go up

In the Christian story God descends to re-ascend. He comes down; down from the heights of absolute being into time and space, down into humanity... But He goes down to come up again and bring the whole ruined world up with Him. One has the picture of a strong man stooping lower and lower to get himself underneath some great complicated burden. He must stoop in order to lift, he must almost disappear under the load before he incredibly straightens his back and marches off with the whole mass swaying on his shoulders...

In this descent and re-ascent everyone will recognize a familiar pattern: a thing written all over the world. It is the pattern of all vegetable life... It is the pattern of all animal generation too.

Descent of Jesus Christ into Limbo,
JACOPO BELLINI (1400–70)

There is descent from the full and perfect organisms into the spermatozoon and ovum, and in the dark womb a life at first inferior in kind to that of the species which is being reproduced: then the slow ascent to the perfect embryo, to the living, conscious baby, and finally to the adult. So it is also in our moral and emotional life. The first innocent and spontaneous desires have to submit to the death-like process of control or total denial: but from

that there is a re-ascent to fully formed character in which the strength of the original material all operates but in a new way.

Death and re-birth – go down to go up – it is a key principle. Through this bottleneck, this belittlement, the highroad nearly always lies.

≈ *MIRACLES*

[61]

Screwtape on Love

The Enemy's demand on humans takes the form of a dilemma; *either* complete abstinence *or* unmitigated monogamy. Ever since our Father's first great victory, we have rendered the former very difficult to them. The latter, for the last few centuries, we have been closing up as a way of escape. We have done this through the poets and novelists by persuading the humans that a curious, and usually short-lived, experience which they call 'being in love' is the only respectable ground for marriage; that marriage can, and ought to, render this excitement permanent; and that a marriage which does not do so is no longer binding. This idea is our parody of an idea that came from the Enemy...

The whole philosophy of Hell rests on recognition of the axiom that one thing is not another thing, and, specially, that one self is not another self. My good is my good and your good is yours. What one gains another loses... 'To be' *means* 'to be in competition'.

Now the Enemy's philosophy is nothing more nor less than one continued attempt to evade this very obvious

Evening Encounter,
THEOPHILE-ALEXANDRE STEINLEN (1859-1923)

truth. He aims at a contradiction. Things are to be many, yet somehow also one. The good of one self is to be the good of another. This impossibility he calls *love*, and this same monotonous panacea can be detected under all He does and even all He is – or claims to be... He claims to be three as well as one, in order that this nonsense about Love may find a foothold in His own nature.

≈ *THE SCREWTAPE LETTERS*

Acknowledgements

The Editor and Publishers are grateful for permission to use the following material, which is reproduced by permission of the copyright holders.

The Letters of C.S. Lewis, Letters to Malcolm, Chiefly on Prayer, Reflections on the Psalms, Surprised by Joy and *Till We Have Faces*, and the essay and poem 'Hedonics' and 'Joy' are reproduced by kind permission of Harcourt Brace & Company.
The Great Divorce, Mere Christianity, Miracles and the essays 'Membership' and 'The Weight of Glory' are reproduced by kind permission of HarperCollins*Publishers*.
They Stand Together and the essay 'Scraps' is reproduced by kind permission of Curtis Brown Ltd.
The Pilgrim's Regress and the essay 'The Language of Religion' are reproduced by kind permission of Wm. B. Eerdmans Publishing Co.

All items are the copyright of C.S. Lewis Pte Ltd.

Full details of the writings of C.S. Lewis can be found in
C.S. Lewis: A Companion and Guide by Walter Hooper,
published by HarperSanFrancisco in 1996.